IF ONLY I KNEW...

By

DeLisha D. Sylvester

Dedication

I dedicate this book to any woman who has ever had a dream but had no idea where to start. Thank you for taking that leap of faith!

Acknowledgements

For starters, I can't believe that I completed this book. To finally come to the end is phenomenal. I often thought there was no way I could write about my entrepreneurial journey. My only hope with this book is that my stepping-stones can help someone else.

I have to start out by acknowledging and thanking God. Thank you for the visions you constantly bestow on me. I know I don't always listen, but I swear you have taught me so much in this past year alone.

Next I'd like to take time to thank my family. Thank you to my fiancé Glenn Tapscott who kept me focused and laughing on those nights where I just wanted to shut down. Thanks for being both mom and dad on the days when I just couldn't.

Thanks to my parents, Diane and Jacob Sylvester. Even though you always feel like you're the last to know about my newest creative adventure, I promise it's always worth it. Thanks for instilling in me the determination and drive I have today. Looks like all that homeschooling paid off.

I would also like to thank some people that, although they aren't blood related, have become family. Derricka Brewer, thank you for being my unofficial official babysitter! Thanks for being my friend and my listening ear when I needed to vent my frustrations. I don't know what I'd do without you.

Thank you to William Tony Epps, my friend, confidant, and overall business brainstorm partner. All of those late night

Facebook messages, brainstorming lunch sessions, and encouraging emails have paid off. I am proud to see you going after everything you want in life. I love that we are both walking in our dreams side by side.

To my team, what an amazing help you've been. The ideas you all come up with are amazing, and I love to see your creativity shine.

I'd like to truly thank Shannon Clark for the amazing design work. I am so happy we were able to connect!

Last, but not least, I'd like to thank the most important person of all. She is the reason this entire journey started. Thank you for scaring the living daylights out of me by being born. Thank you for always offering a hug and kiss when I'm tired. Thanks for cuddling and watching

Caillou with me or else I'd have no excuse for watching it. Thanks for just being you, my little determined, outgoing, sweet and sometimes sneaky little love of my life.

This book is dedicated to you Little Miss Leah Jordan Tapscott. *Mommy loves you!*

Table of Contents

Prologue

"For anyone who has ever had a vision for something greater than themselves."

~ DeLisha Sylvester

I am going to be honest with you. When I set out to write this book, I didn't want to. And, by no means do I consider myself the spokesperson for all entrepreneurs starting out in business. I just want to share the experiences I have gone through. After internally debating with myself, I decided my message could probably help someone.

At the end of this process, I can honestly say that I am not looking for accolades or even, "Kudos, DeLisha." Instead, I decided to write for any woman out there who believed in something

greater than herself, the woman who,
beyond the 9 to 5, knew there was
something else that God expected her to
become. These are the women who didn't
ignore their destinies but instead
embraced them. They are the women
who, beyond a shadow of a doubt,
pushed past the tears, pain, and their
setbacks to attempt their dreams. They are
the women who know within their hearts,
their dreams are something the world
needs.

My chapter as an entrepreneur in
the book of life has just begun. Every day I
am leaping into the unknown, never sure
about where my feet are going to land.
Am I scared? Try petrified. I have my days
where I doubt myself, but I think we all do. I
just take it one day at a time.

What I can say is that I am striving

every day to help in the movement of building stronger and more determined women. No matter what I do in life, my goal is to help other women see their potential. I may never have a nationally known name or face, but that doesn't even matter. I am not looking for fame because it fades. I want to be remembered for my passion for helping women, both young and old, realize that they have the ability to do something amazing in life. If I am able to do that for just a few women, then that is my perfect validation.

I want to be able to say that I tried to leave my mark on this world instead of *I thought about leaving my mark*. I want to show young women that though it may not be easy, they can create their own lane in life and do well. I want the next generation to see that after they get their four-year degree, they may have to face the reality that their hearts might not be cut out for the 9 to 5 scenario; if having a 9 to 5 is your dream, that is okay too, but if you have a dream, you have an obligation to pursue your dream. You have an obligation to the generation after you to be an inspiration and not a fool. The glitz and glamour of fame, although nice, fade and sometimes more quickly than you might expect. Dream big, but beyond that, make those dreams a reality and never let anyone tell you it's impossible.

I was never sure where I'd want to end this book. It's funny that my prologue sounds more like an ending message than the beginning, but my passion for inspiring is much bigger than me. So with this book, I share my lessons, my failures, and my advice.

You don't have to take my advice, but I appreciate you for reading it. Since this is my journey and I am only at the beginning, I will call this part one of my journey. As always . . . Happy Reading!

DeLisha Sylvester

CHAPTER ONE

My Vision

"Ever had a moment where all you could see is where you would be ten years from now?"

~ DeLisha Sylvester

As I embarked on my journey as an entrepreneur, the one thing I can recall those in my circle saying to me was that what I was building was bigger than just me; I was building something bigger than I could have ever thought it would be. They all urged me to stay on my path, even when I wasn't sure of myself. What they didn't seem to understand was that their proclamation about what I was doing confused me then and often confuses me now. As I heard their thoughts and feelings about my entrepreneurial path, I couldn't help but wonder what they were seeing that I wasn't. My vision for what I want was, and still is to some extent, clouded. Often, like many business owners, I've had to ask myself, *Why am I doing this? What does it matter?* and *Is this something that is truly needed?*

At the end of the day, I can honestly say I don't have the answers. I've learned to accept the days when everything is looking up and I am feeling great, but I've also learned to handle the low days when I am wondering how I am going to continue on this path.

One of the first things you will realize about being an entrepreneur is that your mood will change like the weather. When you are building a brand or, in my case, a legacy, you must realize that it takes a lot of mental power. You have to develop a thick skin when things don't work out. I won't lie to you and tell you that I've figured out how to combat all the emotions. What I can say is I am staying true myself and my path.

As I sat down today to write this, I must admit that it was an "in between" day for me. I am excited to share pieces of my journey with others, but at the same time, I wonder how it will be received. I wonder if it will be something that will touch your heart. I wonder if it will inspire you to go after something that you've been putting on hold. I wonder if it will be viewed as every other book out that there that talks about being an entrepreneur and what it takes.

So, as I sat down to write about my journey as an entrepreneur, the first question that I battled with was, "Why would anyone want to hear my story?"

My story is a story that consists of being a mother, a fiancé, a fulltime 9 to 5 worker (at the time), a daughter, a friend, an owner of not one but two businesses (both in their second year in business), and by the end of the book, a fulltime entrepreneur. After I finished laying out all the reasons why I wasn't qualified enough to give advice to other women, I chuckled.

I thought back to the many nights of conversations with other female entrepreneurs that have resulted in businesses started, new visions for existing businesses, and just the feeling of sisterhood that comes from sharing our stories. I realized in that moment that though I may still be unclear about my vision and how it is being seen in the eyes of the public, there are those who understand my goals and are awaiting my thoughts.

Where do I belong?

As a "baby" entrepreneur amongst many great women in business, I often found myself getting lost in the shuffle. I soon realized, "Who am I to say that I am less qualified to talk about my experiences?" No one knows me better than me but God. Some of the best help comes from those who speak from the heart. I began to tell myself, "Self, this book is not to prove that you have all the answers." Heck, if anything, I decided to write this book to share my failures and showcase my missteps in order to help someone else. I decided that it was time to put my life on display and share my truth.

As I sorted through my feelings of being unsure of my own self-worth, I realized that these feelings could not just be feelings of my own. I soon realized that there were other women out there also doubting themselves, pushing their dreams to the side, and not living their lives to the fullest potential. Why? In their minds they may not feel as "qualified" as the people next to them.

So, with shaky fingers and many deletions, edits, copies, pastes, and rewrites, I sat down to bring my journey to life within this book. I decided to be the woman who says, "Hey, I may not know everything, but let me tell you what I *really* didn't know." The goal of this book is to motivate, to inspire, and to push others to push past their current existence.

Sometimes knowing that there is something more for you than what you are doing is a heavy burden, but instead of wondering *why me?* you can rest in knowing that God makes no mistakes. Your life is your life because only you can bear it. You were the only one meant to experience the lessons and trials you've endured in life because they were made just for you.

With that in mind, I ask you to push through. We all have days where we are unsure. I know that there will be times where you look at your path and say to yourself, "I could be doing something else." You'll have days where you will say, "I could be on a beach somewhere or hanging out watching the latest reality show." I've been there, but I can honestly say there is no way that I could live with myself without knowing that I gave up my dreams. There will be time for TV later. There will be time for vacations and relaxation. If you plan it right, you don't have to give up any of that.

Start out by taking a deep breath. Don't worry about the unanswered questions or the doubts circling your mind. Those things are meant to keep you complacent. What you should realize by now is that once you have a vision, it will never fade away. That hunger for seeing if it will work will never stop. It will be a nagging reminder every time you choose to do something other than what you're destined to do.

I know you're saying in your head, "DeLisha, but what if I don't have a plan?" That's fine, neither did I. Just go off of your instinct and courage. Eventually, it will fall into place.

Stop dreaming, start doing.

Act one, scene one. Can I just say I never wanted to own my own business? At twenty-five years old, my plan was to climb the corporate ladder, make close to six figures, and live in a decent home with three kids, a husband, and no pets. I didn't ask for much. When I got the urge to start my first business, I knew a lot of people were looking at me like I was crazy.

Those closest to me wondered what my plan was, especially after coming out the gate as the owner of a bookkeeping business and then casually strolling my way over to the magazine world. I knew it seemed strange. I got a lot of side eyes like, "what are you doing?" and "how do these two things even relate?" To others, it seemed as though I was searching for myself but wasn't having any luck. Little did they know, I wasn't happy; I knew it long before I started my first business, which is why I started my entrepreneurial journey in the first place!

The easiest way to put it is that I was simply tired. Now I know you're saying, "What does a twenty-five year old know about being tired?" Well, I was indeed tired. I knew the value of working in the 9 to 5 world because I had been working in an office setting since I was sixteen, and I was tired. The politics bored me, the money was not coming fast enough, and I found myself feeling trapped.

With the feelings of being trapped combined with the leftover hormones of pregnancy, I decided to start my own business.

CHAPTER TWO

All That Glitters Isn't Gold

*"Bright lights and cha-ching sounds
don't always make for a happy heart . . ."*
~ DeLisha Sylvester

The Beginning.

My big push to start my own business
came in the months after the birth of
daughter. When she finally appeared in
this world on December 22, 2011, I was
petrified. When I returned to the workforce
after a three-month maternity leave, I had
the great idea to start on my master's
degree. I think the month and a half of
bed rest before my maternity leave
actually commenced caused me to
reevaluate what I wanted to do with my

life. At that time, it did not include going back to my current working situation.

Once my daughter was born, I began sending out my résumé left and right, and I almost had a job offer on the table. I had fallen all the way in love with this possible job. With this position, I would have been moving into more of a managerial role. I would have had better hours, which would have been great for sleep and bonding with the baby. Last, but not least, the money would have indeed been right. As you can likely tell, that didn't go through, so my next thought was to gain some more knowledge by going back to school for my master's degree. Big mistake! Don't get me wrong—it is okay to gain more knowledge and go back to school for something you are truly passionate about, but at that time, it was not for me. Between juggling a new baby, my fiancée duties, and the need for sleep, it just wasn't working. I quit my master's degree program after the second semester. The funny thing about it was that I ended up earning a 3.0 GPA, but that didn't matter. The requirement to maintain a 3.0 or higher every semester just proved to be too much.

At that point in my life, I began to realize that I was attempting to combat what I like to call my "mid-20s crisis," but school was just not the answer. As much as I enjoyed my four years of college, college didn't need to be a part of my life at that time. By *enjoy*, I mean that I enjoyed the recreational activities during college. Don't get me wrong, I loved my B.A. in English, which should totally explain how I ended up running a magazine, but we'll get to that later.

Before I decided to quit graduate school, I pondered what I would do with these feelings of "needing more" out of life. Let me tell you what helped me decide my next steps: I saw my check after they added my daughter to my health plan. Yes, ladies and gents, it was that simple—my check had gotten smaller and my bills had gotten larger. So, in April of 2012, I made the decision to start my first business in bookkeeping. My 9 to 5 "job" was as a bookkeeper and program manager. I began working at the age of sixteen in the accounting/administration industry. It was something that I was good at. It was something that I had seen my parents do for a number of years. For my parents, getting into the government was the goal so that I would have a pension when I retired. Although I never made it to that goal, I am happy to have the skills I do because those skills are what prompted me to start my own business. It only made sense that I start my first business in bookkeeping because that is what I had been doing for several years.

I knew that my goals for my bookkeeping business were different than just helping a company with its books. I set my sights on the small business owners and the one-woman and one-man shows. Why? Well, at this time in my 9 to 5 life, I worked for a Chamber of Commerce. A Chamber of Commerce has a role to serve as a connector between businesses and their customers. They also help businesses network and use the services of each other. As I worked there, I realized that many of the chamber members were, in fact, small business owners. Therefore, I put two and two together and came up with four. It only made sense that I appeal myself to small business owners. I also knew that I wanted to educate those who didn't understand the difference between a bookkeeper and an accountant, and I wanted to show them that taking care of their books didn't have to seem like a daunting task.

I was all about educating business owners on their finances, making sure they realized that it wasn't a task that would go away, and that it would cause problems if not properly handled.

To me, all of this made sense. I was working in my field, working for myself (after hours, of course), and earning some extra money doing it. Everything was great until I realized I was beginning to dislike it. Why I didn't see how this would happen escapes me to this day. Sure, I enjoyed meeting with potential clients and talking to them about their business. Offering advice and training clients was the highlight of it, but there were two problems. Problem number one: I did this all day, every day at my 9 to 5 job. It was driving me crazy to look at numbers at work then turn around and look at numbers at home. Problem number two: I enjoyed talking with each client and potential client about their journey as an entrepreneur more than actually doing their work. It was almost as if I was interviewing them on their life in every conversation.

As I began networking more, I met a lot of different women. I soon realized that each of them had incredible stories, and it was then that I realized that I needed something different. At that time, I didn't know what that was, but I knew I needed a more creative outlet, and I needed it fast. I honestly think this was God planting a seed

in my head before giving me the vision that would eventually lead me to start *WE Magazine*. Before that could happen, I would have to learn quite a few lessons.

Wet Behind The Ears.

When starting out, I was what they would call "wet behind the ears." I was so excited to be starting my own venture that I could hardly contain myself. With no plan in sight, I began Facebook networking. I should actually call it Facebook "stalking" because I added every business owner I could think of on Facebook. This, for me, proved to be successful because it connected me to influential women who would later help shape my mind and tactics as a business owner.

Through Facebook, I was able to build a network for my bookkeeping business, secure a logo designer, and build my initial website using Vistaprint. Once I had a logo and a site, I put an ad out on Craigslist for my bookkeeping services and got my first hit. The only issue was that I didn't drive. No license equals zero wheels. I then went back to the drawing board, revamped my business, and began marketing myself as a virtual bookkeeper. This proved to be a great idea because it allowed me to connect with people outside of my region.

Some of the things that I thought about while cultivating my business were:

- To whom do I want to market?
- What do I want to offer?
- What are my limitations?
- How am I going to get my information to potential clients?

Within my first two months, I had my first two clients. Let's pause for the celebration. I think everyone goes through a point when they first start out where they wonder if they will be able to get clients, especially in a service or product-based industry. Once I secured my first two clients, I realized that I had forgotten one key element: I didn't have the slightest clue what or how to charge them. Though I worked as a bookkeeper during the day, I felt that since this was a solo venture, I needed to remain low in price. During that time, I gave a lot of my hours away for free or for less than what they were worth. My hourly billing rate was $10 to $15 an hour.

As I look back on it now, I realize that I wasn't valuing my expertise nor was I valuing the expertise of others in the field. The fear of gaining clients in the beginning really made it hard to properly charge clients. I now realize that it is something we all go through, but we have to be honest with ourselves about it.

My suggestions regarding what to charge are as follows:

- First, start out charging what you are worth and what your work is worth. Don't undercut. It does a disservice not only to yourself, but also to the other people in your field.
- Make sure that you are appealing to the right market. If you are targeting those who can afford your services, they will buy into you if they want to.
- Realize that compatibility is a huge part of the deal. At the end of the day, the person has to like you. They have to want to spend time with you on whatever project you are working on. Be as humble as possible because a funky or dishonest

attitude will overshadow the possibility of getting a lower cost any day.

Determining your worth is always tricky. One of the things I had to realize is that you have to research your field. You have to find out what others are charging. You have to find out what you can do differently that justifies your price. Lastly, you have to be true to yourself.

All That Glitters…

At this point in my business, I had a few clients under my belt and was beginning to realize that by undercutting myself, I had attracted a few not so nice clients. There's an old saying that "you get what you pay for," and it is just as true in reverse. It was as if my once sweet and thankful clients had turned into nightmarish blood-sucking creatures. This was not every client, but there were a few.

I started avoiding emails because of the demanding and sometimes disrespectful things I'd read. I really began to realize that bookkeeping wasn't for me when I received a truly disrespectful email from a client. Not only did she question my integrity, but she also questioned my work ethic. Why, you ask? She didn't like her bill. She had no issues with the work done, but she didn't like the price tag. Now, mind you, I was charging about $10 an hour, and at eight hours for the month, you do the math. By the end of the back and forth, I was one client short.

Now, why would I share this? Well, it's the truth and you cannot be in business without encountering at least one unruly client.

Now that we've cleared that up, I really told this story in particular to say that I learned a lot. I learned when enough was enough for me. I learned when I was tired of pursing a business only for profit, and I learned that if you market to and accept those who jump on low price deals, you will get low price people. You must always remember that running a business is not just about making money. It is about enriching the lives of others around you with the gifts you've been given.

Honestly, I was thankful for that experience because it allowed God to speak to me and show me my true path— one full of longer nights but a much happier and more passionate me.

Know Yourself...

"Sometimes it's better to look inside for the answers. Often there's too much

chatter going on in the world."

~ DeLisha Sylvester

I wanted to leave a legacy for my daughter, but I realized that bookkeeping wasn't it. It was great for extra monthly cash, but I wasn't completely satisfied. I must admit, I enjoyed teaching people how to track their finances, but it still didn't feel like the right fit.

So, one night, God came to me in a dream and said, "DeLisha, remember that English degree? It wasn't just for show or to automatically get you in the door for interviews."

I answered back, "I know, but I don't want to write a book."

He answered me with three words, "Start a magazine."

I awoke from that dream, jumped up, grabbed my phone, and begin typing out ideas. I always say, if you want to hear God laugh, try telling Him your plans. I realized then that God had been laughing at me for months. I know it sounds crazy, but once I realized I was walking down the wrong path, I quickly turned around and began my walk with God beside me.

CHAPTER THREE

Unexpected Push

A colleague of mine once said that owning a business is like giving birth to a baby. After all of the pushing, pain, and feelings of nervousness, you finally give birth to something that is not only beautiful but something that is yours. The pregnancy stage of your business gives you the time to develop your target audience, your brand, and your concept. After months and months of your business developing in the womb of your mind, the time comes for you to give birth to your business.

Change of Direction.

When you start a business in one industry, it can lead to God opening up another door. That was what my bookkeeping business did for me. It not only introduced me to key women in my network, but it also helped me figure out my dos and don'ts for business. In addition to that, it helped lay the foundation of my work ethic, as well as show me the "behind the scenes" lifestyle of an entrepreneur.

If you want a true glimpse into the entrepreneurial lifestyle, follow your true passion. There is a distinct difference between doing work that you have to do, that you hate do, just for the money versus doing what you want to do, loving it, and figuring out how it can be a money generator. If you are looking to stumble, fall, and have your heart broken time and time again, continue on the path of business just for profit.

Even in a non-profit, they have a goal to make money for their cause, but it should never be the only reason. Chasing the money will only leave you unhappy, tired, and eventually broken.

Follow Your Vision.

My vision for *WE Magazine* was to create a media outlet for women without a voice who needed to connect to their target audience. Those women who, in their businesses and lives, were doing incredible things, but they were not being recognized outside of their usual circle. I wanted to create a platform that set the stage for positivity, inspiration, and elevation of the mind, body, and soul.

After having the epiphany that I was in the wrong business, from that moment on, I couldn't think about anything but starting a magazine. I didn't have a name or a true concept, but I knew I wanted to inspire and elevate women. I knew that this time was different; I knew that, this time, I truly felt that I was building a foundation for the right dream. From then on, things just started to line up. I knew that I was receiving an unexpected push. Who knew that within the first four months of having my first business I would have already become pregnant with another? No pun intended.

I started my magazine, which, at the time, was just a blog that I had built in a matter of ten days. I had always known that I wanted it to have "elevation" in the title. My first thought was to just call it *Elevation Magazine,* but I quickly decided that having the word "women" in it brought my goal full circle. From there, *Women's Elevation Magazine* was born.

Plan of Action.

Live life with a vision first because plans are made to be changed. With my business, I started with no concrete plan. All I had was a vision so, with that, I began building my website. Over the course of ten days, I sat down and learned Wordpress, which led to changing my website many times before settling on a design. I still had no plan and no idea how I wanted this magazine to change lives; I just knew I needed to do it.

Over the course of couple of months, I felt inspired, discouraged, overwhelmed, and determined to get this project off the ground. Soon after the name, I began scouting and emailing women in my community who I felt were making a difference with their lives. These were women who had an amazing business or were women I felt needed a moment to shine. With those first few interviews, I ended up being a part of a program with an entrepreneur named

Cheryl Wood (of Cheryl Wood Empowers).
This allowed me to have a private
consultation with her. Cheryl sat me down
and talked with me about my focus. She
told me to research what others were
doing in regards to owning a magazine.
She told me that I needed to work smarter
instead of harder. The thing that I really
took away from the conversation was that
I had a great premise but needed to focus
my direction. I needed to understand that
unlike bookkeeping business, this was not
going to be easy.

At that point, my magazine was set
up like a blog, so I attempted to post two
to three times a week. I quickly realized
that was not working smarter. Her advice
helped push me towards changing the
way I was operating my magazine.

From that point on, I started interviewing women and talked with a magazine owner who suggested how I should outline the magazine to create a digital flipbook, so to speak.

In November of 2012, I produced my first issue. The content was awesome—the women I featured had truly phenomenal stories—but the magazine as a product itself was horrible. Design was not my forté. Once I tried and failed at design, a friend of mine, Michelle Hill-Smith (of OnTask Assistants) offered her services as a graphic designer.

By the end of the year, I felt I was finally going in the right direction. It had a look, and I had a vision, my vision. From then on, the rest was history.

With my new business, I began to refocus on finding a network of women I could learn from. I was the newbie, wet behind the ears, and not really sure of what I was doing. Through continuing my "Facebook stalking" I began to grow my network and, eventually, my friendships. I began to realize that only through getting involved in a network of other women willing and able to teach me would I be able to grow.

A lot of us think that in starting a business, we are an island and that our only goal is to take our talents and consistently sell them. Nothing could be further from the truth. Having support can be the difference between sinking and swimming. Remaining isolated doesn't allow for growth. When I say growth, I mean not only self-growth, but also the growth of your business.

In this world of entrepreneurship, you must remember that you need to build a community around you. Once this community sees your genuineness, understands your authority over your talents, and feels your spirit, they will support you. For me, it was through this support that I was able to see that being in business for profit was not only killing my entrepreneurial spirit, but it was also keeping me away from my true destiny.

The reason I tell this story in great detail is because the unexpected push I got allowed me to birth my blessing. That push came from the birth of a child, the birth of a business, and the interactions with other business owners.

You must ask yourself, "Where does my push come from?" You will have to figure out what is pushing you and what it is pushing you to do. Don't ignore the signs and end up pushing right by your blessing.

CHAPTER FOUR

Power of Doubt

'To ask why is human nature. We can't stand the unknown—why do you think we keep reaching for the stars?''

~ DeLisha Sylvester

Gone Hiding! Be Back Soon.

One of the first things I did when I started my business was go into hiding. I hid what I was doing from family and friends because I didn't fully believe in it. Don't get me wrong, I knew it was my passion that drove me to stay up late and push well past my tired eyes, but I didn't fully believe it would work.

I still have my doubts, especially as I shell out hundreds of dollars a month to push towards my goal. I am less of a nonbeliever in myself these days, I promise. Every time I am presented with the opportunity to speak about my business to anyone who will listen, I hear my belief and determination. Every time I am ready to throw in the towel, God finds a way to send an email my way or a phone call from someone who is inspired by what I am doing, and I keep going.

I say all of this to say that non-belief and non-believers will have you giving up right before you are due to receive your blessing. You may be two steps away, but if you let go before it is time, you don't have anyone to blame but yourself.

When in Doubt, Hide Out.

One of the most important lessons I can possibly teach someone is how to keep important things close to your heart. What that might entail is up to you. In my situation, I chose to hide not solely because of my lack of belief but because I am a strong believer in not showing off something that is unfinished. Remember, it is okay to finish last and deliver the strongest product. You must first be able to stand by your brand before you show it to the world. Even if you aren't sure it's really the way to go, listen to that little voice inside you and speak firmly about what you have built.

I started my magazine in August of 2012, but it was December before I shared it with my parents. I knew I would have their support, but I had to be sure of my direction and what I wanted to portray to the world. I had to make sure that I believed in my product enough to share it with those who were closest to me. If your belief in yourself is broken or lacking, it can be hard to commit yourself to a project and believe that it will work. Lack of faith and belief are a few reasons why businesses never get off the ground.

If people were more supportive of their own dreams and understood that it just doesn't happen overnight, there would be a lot more businesses in the world. Instead of killing your dream or someone else's by stifling it with non-belief, keep an open mind, be supportive, and stick with it.

Why?

I think this is a question that runs through an entrepreneur's mind on a weekly, if not daily, basis. I wondered about it constantly because for every dollar I invested into my business, I realized early on that it took away from something I could have been investing in for my household. In the beginning of most business ventures, the initial investment usually comes from your own pocket. If you happen to get an outside investor, thank your lucky stars and budget accordingly. Beyond the financial toll that a business causes, I worried if *WE Magazine* was truly needed. In a world overly saturated with information, I wondered, "What do we need with another magazine? Who would read it? Who would want to write for it? Who would want to be in it?"

Pushing those thoughts to the side, I sat down and thought about the "why" of my business. I came to the conclusion that the reason I wanted to form this magazine was because I wanted to give a voice to the voiceless. I wanted to showcase women who were doing positive things for themselves and their community. I wanted to tell their stories of women overcoming life's obstacles in order to recognize their true purpose.

Lastly, I wanted to be a part of promoting women, inspiring their target audiences to see the woman behind the veil, and elevating the readers' minds, bodies, and spirits through our topics. This became my "why" and later became the magazine's tagline. It was that simple; I wanted people to get promoted, get inspired, get elevated, and I wanted all of the issues to circle around that underlying theme.

Even with my "why" in place, I still had days and weeks where I wondered, "Why am I doing this?" Sometimes, a clear message is only as good as a clear and concise spirit. If your spirit gets attacked and experiences trauma due to self-doubt, it can cause you to get sidetracked from the path in front of you.

During the first four months of owning *WE Magazine*, I have to say that I was truly lost. I had a key concept, I had interesting content, but my spirit was disconnected from my vision. It wasn't until I started to form a team around me that I began to understand the power behind my passion. In life, you must understand the power behind your passion in order to understand God's vision. One moment I will never forget is the re-launch party we had for the magazine in February 2013. I was nervous as to how my peers would receive the direction I decided to take the magazine. In front of a room of over fifty people, I shared my vision, and by the end of night, I had connected with everyone in that room in some way.

For me, it wasn't about the potential business deals that could be made nor was it about the possible financial gains but

Instead, it was about me connecting the audience with the woman behind the magazine. It was important to have them understand my story.

A business started by passion will gain profit because you will do anything you can to figure out how to make it successful. When you are just doing something just for profit, it's so easy to drop it when it doesn't work.

I realized that you should never underestimate the power of your passion. Your passion will keep you up at night, your passion will give you the confidence to share your story in a room full of strangers with no fear of ridicule, your passion allows you to believe in yourself, your vision, and your testimony when no one else will. At the end of the day, your passion for what you do holds the key to how well you do.

Your passion changes you, and it helps you develop skills you didn't even know you had.

Passion Turned Reality.

At this time, I had a few networking events under my belt, but every time I was called to speak about my business, my hands became clammy, my heart would firmly plant itself in my throat, and my head would immediately begin to pound. I'd have to tell myself, "Self, just speak from the heart. It has gotten you this far."

When it came my turn to speak, I would begin to tell my journey. I'd talk about my "why" and what I hoped to do with my business. I'm told that when I speak about the magazine, my eyes light up and my spirit brightens. The skill of speaking is an element to business that is automatic, and it is highly important if you want the audience to believe in the message behind your brand.

Your passion turns you into a speaker, even though you may be the meekest person in the room on the inside. Even though I am petrified when I have to speak in front of crowds or new people, I do it anyway because my passion to stand for my brand and my vision is what drives my "why."

Whenever you stop and wonder, "Why am I doing this?" take a step back and remember your passion first because it is what will drive you to continue. It is your passion that drives you to place yourself in uncomfortable situations. With that passion, those around you will be able to see through to your heart, and the support will be there.

Continued Drive.

"You may not know your destination, but you'll never get there if you don't put the car in drive."

~ DeLisha Sylvester

Along with having an intense passion for your "why," you must also have the drive and conviction to make your dreams a reality. If you don't have enough drive to push yourself when you are at your most tired, you should re-evaluate whether or not what you are putting your efforts into is really your passion.

When I first started the magazine, I was running myself ragged because I wasn't working smarter; I was just working harder. As I started to understand how I wanted to things done, I still had long nights, but I learned when to cut off. My passion pushed me to keep my eyes open when I wanted to sleep. It pushed me to make connections even when I was afraid that I would hear a "no" or, in some cases, never hear anything at all.

It was my passion that pushed my drive, and because of those two things, I stood firm in my belief that I was giving something to the community that was needed.

You must be able to stand firm in your convictions and beliefs about your business. This means that when no one else believes in your dream, you must fuel yourself with your own self-assurance. This also means that you must stand firm in signs of trouble and not run as soon as things don't go your way. If you are prone to run at the first sight of trouble, owning your own business might not be for you. No one will put in as much effort, energy, and belief into your business as you do. You must remember that there are countless others going through the same struggles you are, so you are never alone.

"We're all in this Together…Right?"

It is important to realize that we are all in this together, or at least we should be. I have to end this chapter with this concept because it is so important. When I think of togetherness, I think of one very important characteristic, and that is being *genuine*. That one word means so much. Some people think that the more words you speak, the more genuine you are, but that is not the truth. Whether or not you are being genuine can be seen all the way to the depths of your soul. You may be able to fake it in the beginning, but you best believe others will be able to see through the act.

I believe that I have been able to get this far with my business because I have remained genuine. When I meet people, I truly want to get to know them, not just their brand. I want to develop a friendship and then find ways that we can help each other. People can feel your spirit, and they can tell if you are not only determined, but humble and genuine as well.

As entrepreneurs, keeping this mindset and the feeling of genuineness in your brand is important. I mentioned genuineness first because it is a key element in how you treat others and how willing you are to help others, even if it means you will get nothing in return.

Remember that you were once in the shoes of a "baby" entrepreneur. This should help you reach back and help someone else realize his or her potential. It is important that you do not forget those who may not be at the same level as you but are trying to get there.

To add to the idea of remaining genuine, you must also keep a sense of transparency within your brand. People don't want to hear about your success 24/7. It's not because they are "hating," it's because they want to know what struggles you made it through to get where you are. They want you to be relatable to them and their lives. They want to look at you and say, "If you made it through, why can't I?" If you only focus on the good and never share the trials, how can people learn from you?

CHAPTER FIVE

When One Door Closes . . .

*"Opportunities don't just happen;
there is no such thing as happenstance,
only God, creativity, and hard work."*
~ DeLisha Sylvester

When one door closes, break the
window! You have to be willing to fight in
order to be an entrepreneur. Nothing is
happenstance; everything that happens is
God's will, hard work, and being creative
enough to be different. When life puts up
its dukes and tries to give you the fight of
your life, don't just stand there and take it.
Those outside looking in may not
understand. They may offer their opinions,
but unless they have gone through or are
currently going through the ups and downs

of their own business, it's hard for them to relate.

What you must always remember as a business owner is that if being an entrepreneur were easy, everyone would have his or her own venture. When I was in college, in my senior year, I wanted to pursue journalism, but I found that, due to my lack of internships and credentials, breaking into the field was too hard, so I gave up. It happens. I know giving up isn't the best thing when faced with adversity, but I also think it's one of the things that led me to start my own path. With the addition of wanting to promote other women, I also wanted to give a chance to those people who wanted to be a part of the journalistic world but didn't have the technical experience.

I knew how hard it was to make your way in someone else's vision. Often times, we choose another route because the path we want seems too difficult (hence me having an English degree yet working in accounting).

I think that's why a lot of us start our own businesses. We, at some point, either get tired of walking the wrong path or we get tired of helping someone else walk the path we want for ourselves.

Once you are finally able to break down the door or window, you have to realize that you can no longer stop just because it gets hard. Those of us who own a business understand what you are going through and continue to go through. We understand that there is an emotional and mental side to it that takes a heavy toll.

We understand that there will be days when you wonder if you've made the right choice. Those are called your "it's not going to just be handed to me" days. Your job on those days is to smile even when you feel like there's nothing to smile about. Send positivity, even when you feel like giving up. Your job is to remain an inspiration to your followers and peers. You can have bad days, but your job is to show the truth beyond those bad days. Show those watching that, yes there are bad days, but here is how you can make it through.

One of the toughest times of my life happened during my revamp of the magazine. At that time, I found out that my mother had been diagnosed with breast cancer. I was devastated. We had just finished monumental birthdays, my daughter's first cognitive Christmas, and I was given this news right before the New Year. I felt like someone was stepping on my lungs and I couldn't breathe. I suffered from anxiety and battled with insomnia.

I stayed up later and later because I would wake up in a pool of sweat or I couldn't get to sleep because I'd have a panic attack as soon as I tried. My subconscious was telling me to deal with my fears head on or I was going to suffer in the dream state. I became snappy and angry, but I realized that I had to put on a happy face because, even though my heart was weak, I had a job to do.

I knew that my message via the magazine was taking off and I didn't have time to sulk and stay in an unhealthy state. I say this to say during times of great trials is when you must be your most human self. Be vulnerable and honest, but show the audience that you are living proof of those quotes you post on Facebook and Instagram. I can't tell you to smile if I have a constant frown on my face. Remember to remain genuine. It's okay to hurt, but be hurt and work through it.

Wish It Were Me . . . Mine.

On those days when you are feeling low and you are not where you want to be in your business, you may feel inclined to look at your peers and see all of the wonderful things they have going on and think things like, "Wow, I wish that was me!" Stop thinking that way! You must remember that every successful gain made by one of your peers is a successful gain for you and the entrepreneurial community as a whole. You may now be wondering, "How could that be?" Let me break it down. If the door of something you wanted closes for you but opens for someone else, they may be able to share some insight and advice that can help you. You must remember that their opportunity was not meant for you and that their blessing might not have been a blessing had you received it. Sometimes God gives others the things we've been asking for because they are not meant for us.

We can become so obsessed with what we want that we don't always pay attention to whether or not the thing we want is just a distraction or a true blessing.

The comparing game...

When I first started my magazine, I shelled out a pretty penny trying to make it all that I thought it should be. There eventually came a time, after months of success, where I still thought, "Okay, the magazine looks great, but where are the sponsors? Where are the ads?" I began to get frustrated as I searched other magazines who were at the same starting level as me but had ads and sponsors galore. I began to think, "Well, what do they have that I don't?" I also wondered how they were pulling in some of the celebrity features when I couldn't even get a callback. What I was experiencing was the "it should be me . . . mine" syndrome. I was constantly comparing my stage of the game to those around me without realizing that my path was completely different than those I was comparing myself to. I believe that it is okay to research other players in your field, but don't do it at the expense of your time and sanity.

You have to ask yourself, "Is what I want so bad something that will help the continued growth of my business in the long haul?" If you answer no, it may be something that will ultimately distract you from your goals, making the path to your destination a longer or more difficult one.

One of things many entrepreneurs need to remember is that their peers didn't just receive their blessing. Not only was God a factor, but hard work was as well. In the beginning, you have a vision, but without the hours, the phone calls, or the painstaking commitment, you cannot have a business, let alone a successful one. Don't become blinded by the successes of others because you have no idea what it took to get them there. You don't know their story or what they had to give up in order to receive what you view as their blessing.

Tunneling.

"On the path forward, see nothing but how you can not only reach your goal. Also keep in mind how you can help someone else reach theirs."

~ *DeLisha Sylvester*

In business, you have to have tunnel vision as it relates to the success of others. This means that you must hold steadfast to the direction that God has steered you. Concerning yourself with how other people are doing only allows for more of a distraction. If you can't see the forest, it's because you are too busy looking at the trees. Don't become distracted by what you don't have, what someone else has, or how they got it.

As the owner of a magazine, it is my job to be happy for everyone. All accomplishments being made were, to me, positive additions to the entrepreneurial community as a whole, especially as it related to women. My goal was, and still is, to report the stories of women who had otherwise been ignored by mainstream media. Even if I have been tempted to call it quits or give up because I wasn't where I wanted to be, I couldn't and still can't because I look at all of the women that were, and still are, making it.

Although I have my days where I feed into the comparison game, I always realize that I have to snap out of it. One of the things I have always said is that it truly excites me to see the success of others. This is true because I know that when it is my time to receive my own blessing, I will. I also believe this to be true because as long as there are positive things to report, I will always have something to talk about using the various platforms *WE Magazine* has built.

When the struggle gets real, and it will, you can't give up because you're not where you want to be. None of what you do in business is about you. Your business is not for you: it is for your audience, your consumer, your reader, etc. Your pleasure should and must reside in bringing something to people that makes them happy, that's beneficial, and that helps change aspects of life for others.

CHAPTER SIX

Beware of . . .

The Opportunist.

"Hey girl I was just thinking about you, we have to connect soon . . ."

I hate to be the bearer of bad news, but only when truths are spoken are lessons learned. There are those in the business world only looking to make a name for themselves. *Shocking, right?* Now that the shock of that statement has resonated with you, let's talk truth. It's sad to say that there are opportunists in the world, but we all know that it is true. In some ways, there is a little opportunist in all of us, so let's discuss the elephant in the room. The opportunists often show themselves as genuinely excited for your business, but there is almost always an underlying goal.

As the owner of a magazine, I get tons of emails, messages, and texts from people wanting to be a part of the magazine, wanting the magazine to cover their clients, or wanting me to spend money on whatever it is they are selling. Although I am here to promote positivity, most don't realize that with any business, there are policies and standards. Just like *Ebony, Essence,* and *Black Enterprise,* etc. doesn't just interview any and every one, neither can I.

That doesn't mean that just because I say no now that it will always remain a no, but there is a process. One of the best lessons I've learned is that you cannot work with everyone and that's okay.

As much as I hate to say no to people, especially as it relates to promoting women, sometimes I have to. What you must realize is that who you work with is just as much of a reflection of you as what you do. For example, if you are putting on an event and have been giving 110% of your effort to make your event successful but your caterer half-stepped on the food, it shows. It shows that not only did they not take your business seriously but also that they were just looking for the opportunity to get their name out there.

When I first started out, I was hungry and truly would allow people to be a part of my brand that were just looking for the opportunity to get some shine, and shine is what I wanted to give them. When it came time to promote the fact that they were a part of the issue of the month, you didn't hear a peep. I was devastated. I felt like I had put in all this work to interview them, gathering pictures, typing up the article, editing everything and sending it off to the designer that I paid out of my pocket. Then, when the day came to promote it, it was like mum's the word. I didn't hear a peep except maybe a few retweets or a single random post, but there was no true promotion of the issue or my brand.

I learned from that moment on that business is business. It's giving and it's taking, and if you're taking the shine but not ready to promote, then I have no use for your opportunist behavior. It sounds harsh, but it is the truth. What I would suggest when in business is that you try to surround yourself with people who are passionate enough about your business to give you the best service and promotion possible.

By doing this, you will be able to not only showcase the drive and talent you have as a business owner, but you will also show that you don't accept less than the best.

Not sure what an opportunist looks like? Here are a few tips:

If they haven't invested in your business through promotion or time, they are opportunists. A true business owner will support all positive business ventures no matter who the owner is. So if they sound like, "Hey girl, can you do _____ for me?" instead of sounding like, "Hello, I saw your product and I was interested in doing _____ with you. In exchange, I am prepared to do _____," they are opportunists.

If they are asking for something before giving something, they are opportunists. They are looking to use your talents as a way to climb onto another platform in business. They care about how you can help them and them alone, and that is bad business.

Another trait of the opportunist is not looking to get anything from you financially but instead looking to drain your mental talents. They look to absorb the knowledge you have learned through painstakingly growing your business.

This doesn't mean don't give advice because this is how we as entrepreneurs thrive and succeed, but that does not mean that you must allow those around you to drain you of your gifts. For example, it can sound like this:

"Girl . . . I need some help figuring out _____ and I was wondering if we can sit down and talk."

Now, put that sentence on repeat about fifteen more times. If are you beginning to feel like a coach and that's not your field, maybe there is something to be leery of.

A life coach gives advice and helps others structure themselves so they can be in a better position in life, but here is the kicker: they charge a fee! Go figure! They are using their talents to help others, but they also realize that their talents are not, and should not be, free. So why do you think it's okay to allow others to use and abuse your services or products for free? H&R Block isn't free. Wal-Mart isn't free. They may have deals, but there is always a price. Beware of those who will continue to happily use and abuse your talents without offering anything of themselves.

The Big Talkers.

In business, there are a lot of people who will promise you the world. They promise that if you work with them, they will take your business and soar it to the next level. They know the right things to say, they've been working on their pitch, they know just what your business needs, and they are willing to share this with you, for a fee. These people are called the big talkers. From the outside looking in, they seem to have it all, and they promise they can make your business skyrocket. They may be able to, but there are a few factors you should consider.

- What does their business model look like? Are they producing the numbers that they are promising, and are those numbers proven or just for show?

- Who are their success stories? What does a business look like after working with them? Are they still thriving or struggling to survive?
- Do they work for your business? Do they mesh with you? Can you see a long-term business arrangement with them?

If you find that it seems like you are spending more money on their fees than actually getting a return on your investment, get out before you give up any more of your money. At the end of the day, being an entrepreneur is hard. Being an entrepreneur in the first year of business is even harder. You have to figure out what you should invest in outside of your regular business costs, and that game can go really wrong or really right. I think we've all had a moment in business where we have wondered why we invested into something only to be scarred because we couldn't really explain what came from it.

My advice is for you to do your research, find out all you can, and then figure out if you will be able to properly put them to use for your business. Don't get "catfished." "Catfishing" is when you believe in and fall in love with something blindly without doing the appropriate research before committing yourself. Remember, Google is a powerful and wonderful friend. Also remember that whether a person is a life coach, business strategist, virtual assistant, etc., anyone who comes in contact with your business should be a valuable asset. This also means that you must analyze whether or not you are at the proper stage in your business to properly execute the things they suggest. Don't get overwhelmed or feel obligated to sign on with anyone, especially if you don't see a return on investment.

I can't tell you how many times I have invested in something only to get my feelings hurt and my pockets depleted. When I started out, I began to think that I needed certain pieces in order to run a successful business. I quickly realized that my company obviously wasn't at the appropriate stage to handle what I thought I needed.

I jumped the gun; I allowed the possibility for what could be done with extra effort to overshadow what my business was ready for. Not only did I lose my time, but I also lost my money, and, last time I checked, you can't get either of them back.

One thing you must realize is that you have to be careful with who you allow to touch your dream. You also have to be careful to not get ahead of your dreams because, at some point, you will experience that fall, and it is no fun.

The Start-Then-Stoppers.

Every moment in business creates a new idea, a new venture, with the possibility of adding spice to your business. You must beware of those that come up with a lot of good ideas yet never start or finish the process. They are the ones who bounce a lot of great ideas off of you, but when it comes time to put the effort into it to make it work, they pour on the excuses. As a business owner or someone looking to own his or her own business, you must remember that work is needed in order to get anything produced. Along with work, it takes time. Don't allow the uncertainty of others to drain your work in progress.

I've been there, where you try to help everyone else discover their dreams while you're still struggling to understand and define your own. Stop it! It's only going to take more energy away from your own journey. You can give someone an idea, you can help someone grab hold of something inside of him or herself, but if they aren't willing to put in the required work, you are wasting your time. Point . . . blank . . . period.

You can lead a horse to water, but you can't make it drink. You can brainstorm the best ideas with someone, but you can't make them create. Concentrate on creating your own dreams, and when those who want it are really ready, help them anyway you can.

Your Surroundings.

As an entrepreneur, you have to assess who you allow into your circle. If you are currently stuck in a comfortable space but you recognize that you want to move into something different, you have to surround yourself with others who want to take risks. If you surround yourself with those who have a problem exploring something new, how can you grow? You must realize that your surroundings influence how well you do just as much as what you do.

When I began my business, I had many people I associated with that I couldn't any more. It wasn't because they did anything wrong; it was just because I was changing. I was having an "Oooh, girl, you're changing" moment and you know what? There was nothing wrong with it. It was necessary to cut ties in order to devote more time to my vision. In order to properly focus, I needed to be around others with like-minded behavior.

It was difficult at first, but I began to realize that it was necessary. I would try to find ways to incorporate the old life with the new, but some things just didn't gel. Not everything or everyone is meant to travel your journey with you. You may feel alone at first, but remember that just like the weather changes, so do people, so why not let a new breeze of friendships flow through?

The Reflection in the Mirror.

The person in the mirror the most important person to be aware of because this person will be the one who looks to undermine your every move. Every day you will battle this person's doubts, and it is up to you to keep this person in check. The person I speak of is *you*. Often times, it is not outside forces that undermine you starting or maintaining your own business. It is the act of consistently self-sabotaging. Self-sabotage can be in the uninspiring language you use or trying to skip important steps in business because you want to get to the moneymaking part, but you are able to change the way you view yourself in your business. Remember, Rome wasn't built in a day, so what makes you think that everything will come to you with no struggle or hard work?

Everyone has experienced the moment where uncertainty makes you panic—that moment when you think that this is all just a big mistake and you wish you could rewind time to forget it ever happened. No one wants to fail; no one wants to be told that his or her efforts were pointless. No one wants to waste money on something they aren't even sure will ever bring them a return on their investment. I've been there. When I said every time I wrote a check to something business-related, "I wonder if I should call it quits," I meant it.

Beyond the money, it is hard to keep your mind, heart, and spirit invested in your dream. There will be late nights, nights away from your family and friends, and you may wonder what all this work gets you. When you feel this negativity coming, and when you feel it overflowing out of you, I want you to stop. I want you to stop and just remember that you are stronger than those thoughts. You are bigger than those thoughts, and if you keep going, you will do more than those thoughts could ever stop you from doing.

Don't allow the reflection in the mirror to place doubt in your waterfall. Keep it positive because, at the end of the day, wouldn't you rather live in possibilities than regret?

CHAPTER SEVEN

Image vs. Perception

Image.

Over the course of the past year, I have heard a lot about changing my image to match my brand. Honestly, this never something I thought about. Even though I love my business, I didn't want it to propel myself onto the forefront. I was perfectly happy creating campaigns and thinking of new ways to diversify the business . . . behind the scenes.

The more I went to networking and social events, the more I realized there was something completely different between myself and the other businesswomen.

Apparently my image didn't match the part of a CEO. Don't get me wrong, my closet was filled with cute outfits from H&M and Forever 21. I got many compliments, but once they took a look at my feet, it was like I had broken some secret code. I'm a strong advocate for the "flat shoe movement." I believe in dressing comfortably, not because I am ashamed of my height but mostly because those high-heeled shoes hurt.

Why suffer in pain for an hour or two when I can be comfortable in some plain flats? Flats must send out a warning to other businesswomen that says "inexperienced entrepreneur alert." Some of my closest advisors told me to spruce up my look because, in this game of entrepreneurship, the way you look says just as much about you as the product you produce. Apparently, I didn't come across as the "CEO of a digital magazine publication."

It was now my job to figure out how to balance what people want to see with who I am. I never want to get so glitzed and glammed up that people feel like they can't approach me. It's all about balance and not allowing anyone to define you. Yes, your look should match your brand but only on your terms, never someone else's.

Of course, that doesn't mean it is right for someone to judge you based on your looks, especially not before hearing what you have to say, but it happens. Honestly, I believe those who shut out others based on looks could be shutting out someone who's saying what they need to hear. Not taking someone seriously because their haircut or their shoes is an insult to the person behind the brand. Remember that someone can wear the most beautiful clothing and still have an unappetizing personality. Never judge a person by their outside appearance; instead take the time to read their spirit. You never know, you could be dismissing the next Oprah.

My advice to those who face this same dilemma is not to conform to the stereotype, but to make the stereotype fit into your world. I love a nice outfit as much as the next girl, but what I won't do is look how others want me to. I have added heels to my collection, but they are heels of my choosing (and my height for that matter). I rock what I want. If that means I turn others off, well then it must mean they aren't for me to meet.

Perception.

At the end of the day, image is everything, sad to say. People would, sometimes, rather deal with the person who has the prettier outward appearance than the plain Jane. What you must remember is that even though your outward appearance is the first thing people see, at the end of the day, your voice and actions will overshadow your appearance.

Your image is what they judge you on until you open your mouth, and your image can be a detriment to others wanting to work with you. No matter how great your ideas are, no matter how great your product is, if your image doesn't match, it causes confusion. Is it sad? Yes. Until we change our perception of what is important, nothing will change.

However, it is important to not just look great, not just feel great, but to also *be* a great individual. Image doesn't matter if your attitude is horrid. Once people get past their perception of you, you must back it up with intelligence and humbleness.

When I attended networking events, I would throw on a cute dress, some flats, and rock my little wavy afro. No makeup, no heels, just me. I couldn't promote my business easily because people were so focused on my image. At first, I must admit that I was a little hurt. It was like being in middle school all over again. Soon I began to realize that it's just a part of the game. Once people got past my *al natural* appearance and listened to me, they were truly inspired by what I had to say. They realized my passion for my business because I believed in it wholeheartedly. My passion leaked from my pores, my humbleness poured out in my speech, and I still ended up winning many people over. Did it take a lot more effort? Yes.

For all of those who chose not to hear me because they could only focus on the image, that's okay, maybe it wasn't our time to meet. What I hope is that, one day, those people can move past the outer and hear my soul. If not, "Oh well, honey, you can't win them all!"

This lesson has been the toughest for me to learn and come to some sort of understanding. My business has definitely grown, but I find it hard to reach people on a face-to-face level, at least until they hear me speak. At the end of the day, I say all this to say though I may have increased my list of subscribers or gotten people more interested in my brand, I still have to fight their perception of me.

In the world wide web of life, I was killing it. My image online included a multitude of professional glam shots. For some reason, I realized that, for website purposes, I needed a professional appearance. That meant glammed face and all, yet, for some reason, it didn't translate into real life. What I realized early on is that your image also includes your appearance on the web. Okay, great, so I had one thing accomplished, claps for me. One of the biggest things you can do to help your business is to have a professional picture. I was there once; I get it. Starting out, money is tight. When I first started, my business Facebook account profile picture was of me on the couch, which was cropped out. Thought I was cute, and I was, but professional? HA! Not a chance. I got my first set of pictures done by my third month in business.

As a publisher, one of my biggest pet peeves is to want to feature someone and realize that they have no professional pictures anywhere. How can you claim to be a professional and send me a picture of you chilling at the barbecue or in the bathroom? I'm telling you this because I want you to do better. If money is tight, go to the mall and get in on their specials. Do something! Because just like my in-person image made it hard to explain my business in person, it is even harder to appeal to someone through the web. They can easily just click away from your site and never return.

This brings me to my second point. Invest in a professional website. It's costly but worth it. Again, when I first started out, I

played the build-my-own-website game.
As a matter of fact, I did it twice, but I
quickly realized that it wasn't going to
work. People like things that look good.
They are more likely to buy into and trust a
site that looks crisp and clean than
something thrown together. Remember to
let those that can do, do it. Unless you are
going to take the necessary steps to learn
how to build your website, let the
professionals handle it. You don't have to
be superwoman.

CHAPTER EIGHT

Everyone Has a Message, and Everyone Has a Lane. . .

"Who is your audience?" Everyone.
Well, if everyone is your audience then no
one will hear your message.

~ DeLisha Sylvester

Not everyone is intended to receive your message, which is why we have so many business owners within the same industry. I have had the wonderful opportunity to meet women who own their own magazine, each with a different message behind their brand. Their message was the foundation on which the brand stood. None of their messages were the same. They all had a different starting place and story. Within her brand, each woman shared a little bit about herself through the stories she chose to focus on.

The world of entrepreneurship is a vast one with enough room for many to pursue their passions. You need to focus on your message, your vision, and your brand as a whole. There are many businesses that are in your particular industry, but you should not see them as competition. The idea of competition would mean that you are looking to one up or beat someone else when, in actuality, the only competition is yourself.

You also need to remember that there are many messages, but every person receives them differently. Don't concern yourself with those who may not understand what you are trying to convey. There will always be someone who is in need of your messages.

Concern yourself, instead, with the authenticity and validity of your message as a whole. Are you representing yourself the way you intend? Is your message coherent and concise enough to reach the masses? Is your brand strong enough to live in its own presence?

If you can answer yes to each of those questions, you are in a great space not only to market your business but also to have it market for you. In order to do this, you must first determine your target audience.

When I started my magazine, I wanted it to be something that represented women as a whole. No matter what color, race or creed, I wanted all women to feel welcome to read my magazine. I wanted them to look past the shades of color of the women I featured and get to the true message behind their stories.

We often forget that it is not the color of our skin that defines us but the message we broadcast to the world and the images we portray. Focus on that as a concept and choose to incorporate things in your brand to help to diversify it. Find your niche and make it work for you. Once you've done that, you will be in much better shape to reach others.

CHAPTER NINE

Invest in Your . . .

"If you love it then nurture it and watch it grow…"

~ DeLisha Sylvester

Business.

How can you expect for anyone to invest in your company if you don't. Financially you must invest, spiritually you must invest . . . emotionally and mentally you must invest. Bottom line, you must invest, and yes, you've probably heard this all before, but ask yourself: are you truly doing it?

Everyone wants to know the secret to owning a successful business, and it's quite simple. Your greatest investment in your business is you. Before you hire anyone to help you with your business, you must invest yourself in it and nurture it. You can't pay someone to do something that you can barely articulate. I mean, you can, but it would be a waste of money. In your first year of business, your company is more than likely funded with your own money. Therefore, you can't afford it. You must give your blood, sweat, money, and sleep (*yes, I said sleep*) because if you don't know your business, no one else will.

Team.

Invest in a group of people that will tell you the truth. Having a bunch of "yes men" and "yes women" around is pointless because at the end of the day, it is your company, and you always have the final say. You are your own "yes man" or "yes woman." You need people around that are going to have different incorporating factors. You need people around who are going to tell you when you are reaching or if you are going off the deep end. You need people around you that are going to keep you levelheaded and humble. Lastly, you need people around who are going to tell you that your "stuff" doesn't always smell baby fresh.

Investing in your team doesn't always mean a financial investment. If you have friends you trust to bounce ideas off of, then by all means, invest in them. Invest in them with your time, your love, and your interest in their lives. As business owners, we sometimes forget those around us as we try to build our legacy. Stop that. Don't lose valuable team players because you feel you are too busy to listen and be a part of their life.

Invest in people such as an awesome graphic designer, photographer, mentor, and whoever you need alongside you in order to be successful. As mentioned before, you must invest in people that have mastered what they do. Staying in your lane and directing them with your vision will prove to be more beneficial in the long run.

It is important to understand that though you can do everything you set your mind to, it does not mean you should. When I first started *WE Magazine* and was doing it as a blog, I attempted to build my own website before hiring my website designer. It took me an entire ten days to figure out Wordpress, and even then I was never happy with the website.

I was driving my car in someone else's lane. I attempted to save money by doing it myself. At the time it was a huge mistake because I didn't know enough about web design. Though others told me that it was a great job, considering that I did it myself, I knew the truth. When I decided to change the magazine from blog style to a digital magazine, I also started out doing it myself.

You would have thought I'd learned my lesson, but obviously not! The first issue I created was the November 2012 issue. I honestly feel that I should apologize to those featured because even though I had quality content, my unfinished and poorly done product overshadowed the content.

I was still driving in someone else's lane. Yes, we can all study something and figure out how to do it, but will it "wow" the intended audience? Will they remember you for the final product being well put together or will they remember the poorly done work. See, the thing about your audience is that they are not dumb. They know when you are half-stepping, and they know when you are not staying in your lane. It wasn't until I took the time to hone my website design skills that I felt comfortable doing that portion myself. Even though I can handle any website design myself, I still know my love and where it ends.

If there is one thing that I could share with the readers of this book, it's that though we can do many things, we should stick with the one thing we do well. When too much is added under your umbrella, your business becomes a cluster of half-mastered products. Will people invest in your business? Yes, but they will not stay for the long haul. This is not to say you can't have multiple passions, but with each passion, you have to have the ability to realize when you need help. That help comes in the form of a team. Each person on your team needs to have already mastered their role. If you cannot focus in on your business idea, if you are constantly changing your businesses type, or if you are consistently weaving in and out of your own lane, then owning your own business might not work out for you. Stick first with what you know, what you are good at, and lastly what you believe in.

Once you recognize that staying in your lane is something that you must do in order to create a more valuable you, the better off you will be. Remain focused on what you want and understand that though you might be able to figure it out, sometimes it's best to let others do it!

Network.

One of the most important things when growing your business is networking. So I want to talk about networking and the highs and lows of it all. I've found that since celebrating my first year in business, I have spent a lot of money in this department. I also found that many of the people I networked with had yet to formulate their business; therefore, they sought out network groups to serve as a guide.

This is something that I wish I would have done more of. With husbands, children, and in my case at the time, a full time job, it is hard to do a lot of face-to-face networking. It took me a good six months to find the right network fit for me. I spent money left and right buying into forums that, in the end, didn't keep my attention.

My note of caution to anyone starting a business is to research groups carefully. Even add some of the members from the networking organization on Facebook. All and all, do your homework because no one else can tell you where you fit best. I believe that everyone has valuable information in some way, shape, or form, but not everyone is the right fit to receive that information.

So before proceeding, ask yourself these questions:

- What are they offering for their asking price? (Some groups have associated costs.)
- Does it seem more about getting you to spend your money before getting tips, or is it an inviting community that shares upfront?

- Do you honestly think that you will put in the required effort getting know those involved in the network, or are you just looking for clients?
- Last, but not least, does it feel good to you? The best lesson my mother taught me was to go based off of my internal vibes.

If you are not ready to connect to the person behind the business, then you are not ready to be in business. Also please note that just collecting a lot business cards is not connecting with a business or its owner. Be ready to connect with the person behind the business and not just for possible financial gain! Yes, money is a driving force behind having a business (*you have bills, right?*), but it will not keep you in business. People do not like to feel like they are being sold to. That's why they hang up on telemarketers very quickly. Your best bet at getting in the door with someone is to do something you've done all your life: get to know them first. Get to know your intended network; build a relationship with them and their business.

Invest in Yourself...

Though you cannot physically see your spirit, in a way, it shines through. You need to invest in having a positive mindset that believes in your product, that is honest, and is really geared toward helping others. Remember to show it by killing them with a smile. People talk about the good, the bad, and the disingenuous behavior of those around them. It's important to portray and act on actions that are truthful.

The biggest piece of the puzzle is you. You have to invest in yourself, which means cutting off from your business. It is important to realize how well your body and mind function as you open yourself to more responsibility within your business. At the end of the day, you cannot allow your business to run you.

Invest in your relationships.

One of the toughest things that you will have deal with in business is maintaining and possibly letting go of your relationships. Once you become an entrepreneur, life as you know it changes. A new addition appears in your life, and though it may not come in the form of a bouncing baby boy or girl, it will definitely need the same kind of nurturing and care. Once you accept and realize this, you should begin to see a change in your priorities.

I think back to a conversation I had

with my fiancé regarding our relationship and business. He expressed that he was nervous about my business. At that time, he was thinking about going back to school, as well as dealing with the possibility of adding more to his work schedule. e worried what all the changes would possibly do to our relationship. As I sat there, I could see the distress in his face.

I calmly explained to my fiancé that all we could do was try. We both come from marriages lasting fifteen plus years, so we have some pretty long records to beat. I realized early on that he was the one for me, and because of that, I wanted him to be successful in whatever he wanted. See, I want him to venture off and do everything that makes him happy. I realize that I would not have been able to pursue any of this without the days where he took over and played both mom and dad.

A word of advice: don't be greedy. Allow your partner to explore things that makes him or her feel validated. One of the reasons I started my businesses was so that I could leave my child a legacy. I also began to realize that I was starting to lose my own identity. I was starting to become just "Leah's mom" or "Glenn's fiancé," and while all of that was peachy, I needed something that would take me out of my element. Outside of just going to work every day and coming home to take care of my family, I knew I needed a positive outlet. I say all of this to say that just as much as I needed an outlet, so did my significant other.

Balance is about more than cutting off from your business and spending some much needed personal/family time. It's also about balancing your wants and wishes with the wants and wishes of your partner. If your partner begins to feel like your business is overshadowing the family ties, then you seriously need to reconsider some things. Yes, it's going to be a bumpy road, especially as you take on more and your family dynamics change, but no business venture is more important than family. Period!

Friendships.

You also need to invest in your friendships in the same way you invest in everything else. The same people you were with before you started your own business may not be the same people who stick around. It's a sad fact, but sometimes a good thing. Some of your friends may not understand your newfound love for networking events and staying up until the wee hours of the morning working on your business. Some of them may not understand the passion you have for getting involved in entrepreneurship, and guess what? That's quite all right. Being an entrepreneur is not for everyone. Some people would rather club than produce something long standing and valuable to the community.

Some people would rather sleep than attend an event that can potentially connect them with the right people for their business. Some people would rather vacation than pay for a team to help take a dream and turn it into reality.

When you start to realize that those "friends" that were there before your entrepreneur days started are starting to disappear, don't fret. It is what it is, and in order to build a strong foundation, sometimes you have to replace some of the older bricks. In order to ensure that you get to your destination, sometimes you have to upgrade the parts of your car.

Think about it this way, if you've had the same engine for years and it is starting to give out, what should you do?

- Spend a bunch of money repairing or
- Invest in something more durable and get credit for your trade-in

If you're smart, you'll do the latter. It doesn't mean that you loved that car any less because you had to let it go. It just means that you realized that in order to safely and surely get to your destination, you had to upgrade.

You must also realize that you have no room for any extra negative energy around you. You already have to deal with your own self-doubt. Why add to that by having non-believers in your circle? Once you let a lot of that dead weight go, you will make room for the friendships you will inevitably gain from being in business. Remember that building a relationship within the entrepreneurial community will help you not only navigate its waters but also align you with those who can eventually help you.

I lost a lot of friends when I started my business, partially because I just couldn't deal with the crazy and partially because when I dive into something, I dive full force, headfirst. Those who understood what I was trying to do eventually understood that I was a woman with a mission and a purpose. They too were going after their own dreams; therefore, we would eventually reconnect.

CHAPTER TEN

Stress

"If you don't control your stress, it will control you."

~ DeLisha Sylvester

Handling stresses in your business is important to your health and business success. Why business success? Well, if you are dealing with a situation that is causing you stress, guess what happens? Your business productivity slows down because you're too busy worried about that situation.

My recommendation is to cut out your stress. If it's old friends who don't understand your new grind, you may have to put them on the back burner and return when they get a clue. When those around us aren't happy with their current situation, they can sometimes give off negative energy, which, in turn, can cause stress to those around them.

It's understandable that as entrepreneurs, many of us started our businesses to change our current situation because we weren't satisfied. But there are those of us who complain and maintain our current position, and then there are those of us who defy odds and push through in order to get something better. You have to ask yourself which will you be.

Subconscious Stress.

"We are all failures at something. It's whether or not we choose to stick with that title that defines us."

~ DeLisha Sylvester

Subconsciously, you may be deliberately attacking yourself. Ask yourself three simple questions.

- Do you still take care of tasks that could easily be delegated to someone else?
- Are you finding it hard to shut off and focus on family without feeling like you're sabotaging the growth of your business?
- Do you constantly find your scheduled "me time" becoming shorter and further between?

If you answered yes to any of these questions, you are subconsciously sabotaging yourself and, thus, inducing stress.

We all know that late nights and entrepreneurship go hand and hand.

There comes a time where you have to shut down, but if you're at the point where the only times your family sees you are when you are pushing them off to work or school or putting them to bed at night, you have a problem. Balance is the key, and without it, stress will consume you. With stress comes negative thinking, and with negative thinking comes self-doubt, which can ultimately tear your business apart before it even gets off the ground. I am telling you this because we all do it, even me. After all these years, I still do some of these very things. I won't lie to you; I want to be straight up and honest. It's hard to stay motivated. In order to stay positive, I think back to my audience. They are the reason I keep pushing because I know that they are being inspired by the messages. It's little things like that, that can help those long days seem shorter.

CHAPTER ELEVEN

Life Goes On...

"Though we'd love it to slow down, even for just a second, the world keeps moving."

~ *DeLisha Sylvester*

I wanted to talk about my life for a minute. When I started this book, I had a full time job. I would get up at 7:00 am to feed and dress my child. I would get dressed, and be out the door by 8:00 am. Off to the metro I would go where I would ride a thirty to forty minute train into DC. I would get to work, and there I sat until 5:30 pm. Then I got back on the train, walked home, fed my child, played with my child, and began to take out dinner to cook. By then, it would be about 7:40, but we weren't eating until 8:40. By the time I ate and got my child ready for bed, it would 9:00 pm. Was my day over? Absolutely not! I continued to spend the next three to four hours working on my passion. I could be sending emails, answering emails, typing up interviews, listening to a podcast, and sometimes conducting interviews. Many people asked me when I would sleep. That's a good question. I got in the bed around 11:30 or 12:00 a.m., but I may not fall asleep until 1:30 am.

Why, you ask? The answer is a simple one . . . my brain needs to unwind, and what better way to unwind than reading emails from your phone? That leaves me about six hours of sleep, which is more than a lot of other entrepreneurs I know, but still not enough. All that leads to a restless mind full of stressful thoughts, which leads to an undernourished body. It sounds crazy, but I'm probably not half as bad as some entrepreneurs who never sleep. The amount of pressure we place on ourselves to get things done and succeed in making the most out of each day begins to take a toll on our minds. What I suggest is to set goals for yourself that you hope to complete, but if everything doesn't get done, don't stress about it. Worrying will do nothing to get those goals completed faster. I say all this to say I wish life would slow down sometimes, but it doesn't work that way.

Things You Cannot Change.

Earlier in this book, I mentioned the time my mother was diagnosed with breast cancer. Talk about a new year, a new business, and a new set of stress. As I stressed myself out regarding her health state, I began to develop more and more panic attacks. This meant less and less sleep due to waking up in a pool of sweat. I started to wonder if I was doing everything I could for her.

I'd question if my business was a waste or if I should stop and pay more attention to her. Something tells me she would have killed me if had I stopped. My mother is never one to allow me to quit when her health issues arise. Still, all of these things ran through my mind. I went into a state of numbness and anger. Snapping at work, at home, I was angry. From the business view, I may have seemed together, but it was hard. I was working overtime trying to distract myself from the problem. Combating migraines and sleep deprivation with Aleve and mountains of caffeine, I realized this simple

fact: *there was nothing I could do about it.*
Life goes on.

As much as I wanted to take her cancer away, I couldn't, but what I could do is everything I could to take care of myself. Accepting that I couldn't change things was the first step. The second was to stop drowning myself in my work. It wasn't helping. It was keeping me distracted, but it wasn't helping.

As entrepreneurs, we must realize that there will be things that we cannot change, both professionally and personally. We cannot allow ourselves to drown. For starters, our bodies won't allow us to. Secondly, God doesn't place anything on us that we can't handle. Remember, at the end of the day, you were built to withstand what you are going through and a heck of a lot more.

CHAPTER TWELVE

Message from the Founder

"Your gain comes after sweat, tears, and a little pain . . ."

~ *DeLisha Sylvester*

There are truly no handouts in the entrepreneurial world. You are more likely to be given a chance in Corporate America than working as an entrepreneur. If you're looking for an easy way to make money, pack up your stuff and exit, stage left.

As a founder, owner, CEO, or whatever you want to call yourself, you must realize that you will work harder than you have ever worked in Corporate America. Instead of working to get promoted, you work to close the deal. In a Corporate America, if you don't get the promotion, it's okay! You still keep your current level position, but as an entrepreneur, if you don't close the deal, you don't eat; it's as simple as that. However, you must be thankful that you are able to go after your dreams because it is a blessing.

The fact that you've realized the abundance of resources around you is inspirational to others who haven't reached that level in their faith. Be thankful. The fact that you have the ability to fund your business no matter how difficult it may be to write those checks is phenomenal. Be thankful.

I had to write this message because I think that a lot of entrepreneurs forget that not everyone can do what they do.

Entrepreneurship is for those who put in the hard work. It is for those that have the determination to push past life's setbacks and create possibilities. It is for those interested more in the people who use their service/product than the money they might make off the sale.

Remember that though you may not always get a "thank you" or a "job well done," it doesn't mean that no one is watching. That doesn't mean that no one is listening or empowered by your everyday life story, because they are. Your peers are watching, your children are watching, the world is waiting for you to shine. And if a negative wind should blow, know that God controls your sail. No matter what storm comes your way, it will only be momentary. Remember this and always be thankful.

Is This The End . . .?

I start every issue of *Women's Elevation Magazine* with a message from the founder. I feel like this book is just a longer version of that. The point of this book has been to share my entrepreneurial journey thus far.

The point has been to share the lessons I have learned while walking my path. By no means is this the entrepreneurial bible. Don't start sending me letters about how you don't agree *with my truth* because your truth and my truth are completely different.

This book is an ode to entrepreneurship, a compilation of my highs and lows. This book is just my way of saying "I wish I had known then what I know now."

At the end of the day, I'm still learning, still falling, and still building. Honestly, that's all I can do. That's all any of us can do. Giving up just isn't an option. I hope to continue to update you. I also hope that you will allow yourself to figure what you've always wanted to do and go for it. Start small, but at all costs, please start.

~"*A dream is nothing more than a star waiting to shoot across your sky. Instead standing in awe of it, find ways to recreate that magic in your own life.*" ~

DeLisha Sylvester

www.ingramcontent.com/pod-product-compliance
Lightning Source LLC
Chambersburg PA
CBHW051718090426
42738CB00010B/1971